HOT

Celebrity Biographies

Justin Bieber

TEEN MUSIC SUPERSTAR

BY ALLY AZZARELLI

Enslow Publishers, Inc.
40 Industrial Road
Box 398
Berkeley Heights, NJ 07922
USA
http://www.enslow.com

For Andrew Meravi

Library of Congress Cataloging-in-Publication Data:

Azzarelli, Ally.

  Justin Bieber : teen music superstar / Ally Azzarelli.
     p. cm. — (Hot celebrity biographies)
  Includes index.
  Summary: "Find out how Justin became such a huge star. From busking on the streets in Stratford, Ontario, Canada
    and singing on YouTube to getting a record contract and selling out concerts—read all about his life"—Provided by
    publisher.
  ISBN 978-0-7660-3873-8
  1. Bieber, Justin, 1994—Juvenile literature. 2. Singers—Canada—Biography—Juvenile literature. I. Title. II. Series.
  ML3930.B416A99 2011
  782.42164092—dc22
  [B]   2010048126

Paperback ISBN 978-1-59845-287-7

Printed in the United States of America

122011 Lake Book Manufacturing, Inc., Melrose Park, IL

10 9 8 7 6 5 4 3 2

To Our Readers: We have done our best to make sure all Internet addresses in this book were active and appropriate when we went to press. However, the author and the publisher have no control over and assume no liability for the material available on those Internet sites or on other Web sites they may link to. Any comments or suggestions can be sent by e-mail to comments@enslow.com or to the address on the back cover.

♻ Enslow Publishers, Inc., is committed to printing our books on recycled paper. The paper in every book contains 10% to 30% post-consumer waste (PCW). The cover board on the outside of each book contains 100% PCW. Our goal is to do our part to help young people and the environment too!

Illustration Credits: The Canadian Press, Darren Calabrese/AP Photo, p. 29; Charles Dharapak/AP Photo, p. 35; Charles Sykes, p. 43; Chris Pizzello/AP Photo, pp. 4, 16; Evan Agostini/AP Photo, pp. 1, 19, 22, 24, 30; Gerald Herbert/AP Photo, p. 33; John Raoux/AP Photo, pp. 10, 14; LORNVU/SIPA/AP Photo, p. 38; Matt Sayles/AP Photo, p. 40; Peter Kramer/AP Photo, pp. 20, 25; Richard Drew/AP Photo, p. 12; Tim Larson, p. 7; Tammie Arroyo/AP Photo, p. 37.

Cover Illustration: Chris Pizzello/AP Photo
Cover Photo: Justin Bieber at the MTV Video Music Awards with the award for Best New Artist in 2010.

Contents

From YouTube to Big Star

On November 21, 2010, audience members howled and cheered as sixteen-year-old Justin Bieber made music history. Once just a small-town boy from Canada, Justin is the youngest performer to win not just one but four 2010 American Music Awards (AMAs). Upon winning his AMA trophies for T-Mobile Breakthrough Artist, Artist of the Year, Favorite Pop/Rock Album, and Favorite Pop/Rock Male Artist, Justin told CBS News, "I can't stop smiling; this is amazing." Justin's emotional thank you speeches included genuine thanks to his fans, family, and everyone who helped make him the superstar he is today.

After beating out Eminem and his own manager, Usher, for favorite pop/rock male, Justin said, "Truly I don't know how this is possible because I've been singing Eminem since I was three and Usher is my mentor. So this is big." Usher had no hard feelings losing to the youngster. "To see Justin take the award—having received that award before—it was like an out of body experience," Usher told reporters backstage at the award show. "It was emotional. I don't cry

◄ *Justin Bieber poses with his AMA awards on November 21, 2010.*

Full Name: Justin Drew Bieber
Nickname: JB, JBieb, Biebs, or JBiebz
Birthday: March 1, 1994 (Some magazines say March 14; based on Justin's tweets, it's March 1.)
Birthplace: Stratford, Ontario, Canada
Family: Mom, Pattie Mallette, and dad, Jeremy Jack Bieber, divorced when Justin was young. His dad remarried and has two children, Jazmyn and Jaxon.
Instruments He Plays: Piano, guitar, drums, and trumpet

that often, but I did. Hopefully it gives an indication of how hard we worked to build a career that hopefully will flourish and blossom over the years."

But Justin is no stranger to success. He sells out concerts in less than one hour. He was the youngest performer to win an American Music Award for Artist of the Year. As of March 2011, he had more than 8 million Twitter followers. He has performed for President and Mrs. Obama in Washington. His face is everywhere—from Proactiv® commercials to magazine covers all over the world. There are Justin dolls, nail polish, fragrance dog tags, official headphones—even Madame Tussauds wax figures. He's Justin Bieber and he's an international megastar!

MEET JUSTIN BIEBER

Justin Drew Bieber was born on March 1, 1994, at 12:56 A.M. in Stratford, Ontario, Canada (population 32,000) to Pattie Mallette and Jeremy Bieber. His mom wanted to become an actress when she was a teenager. However, her dreams

FAVORITES

Music Artists: Usher (of course!), Justin Timberlake, Drake, Michael Jackson, Boyz II Men

Food: Sub sandwiches, fast-food burgers, and spaghetti

Snacks: Doritos®, ice cream, Hershey's Kisses®, Swedish Fish, and Sour Patch Kids®

Dressing Room Must-haves: According to Sunny Pepper of Examiner.com, "It seems [Justin] just wants concert promoters to outfit his dressing room with mixed nuts, potato chips, herbal teas, vitamin water and deli, vegetable, and fruit platters."

Colors: Purple and blue

Gadgets: iPhone, Blackberry, iPad, and a black MacAir laptop

Clothing: Hoodies, high-top designer sneakers, sunglasses, baggy designer jeans, caps, and slick jackets.

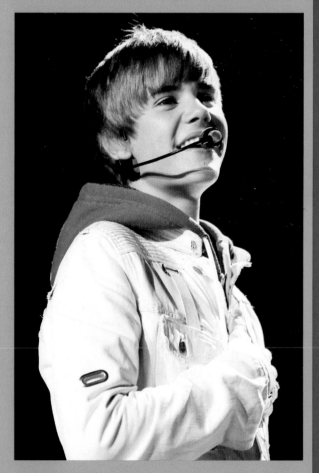

Justin likes wearing hoodies and the color purple.

JUSTIN TALKS GIRLS

In 2011, Justin denied rumors that he was dating Selena Gomez. However, photos and news stories show the two holding hands and acting like a couple. Are they more than just BFFs? Fans are left to decide for themselves.

His Perfect Girl: "A girl has to have a beautiful smile, beautiful eyes and she should have a good sense of humor. She should be honest, loving, and trustworthy."

of acting were put on hold when Justin was born so that she could focus on taking care of him. Justin's parents had him when they were young, and their marriage ended when he was two. Justin visited his dad, but was raised mostly by his mom and grandparents.

"My grandparents mean so much to me and they played a big role in my childhood," Justin told *Life Story* magazine. "My mom and I have always had a great relationship, and my grandparents helped raise me. My dad and I have a great relationship too. My mom did what she had to, to make sure we were taken care of."

Justin and his mom have a very strong faith in God and the church. His hometown church raised money to help Justin's mom buy his first drum set. Justin is grateful for being given the gift of music. "I'm a Christian and I pray before every show and am thankful for every blessing," he once tweeted.

Growing up in Stratford, Justin attended Stratford Northwestern Secondary School in his hometown. Justin learned to speak French in school. It is very common for young people in Canada to speak both English and French. When Justin wasn't attending school, he skateboarded and played soccer and basketball. He loves all sports—he even plays golf! As a true Canadian, Justin is an avid hockey fan, both playing and watching. His childhood bedroom is filled with sports trophies, awards, and ribbons.

In addition to sports, Justin has always loved music. When Justin was a little boy, his mom would listen to R&B music with him. She loved the harmonies from the 1990's group Boyz II Men. His dad, on the other hand, was a fan of rock music. "He's the one who got me into classic rock and then turned me on to stuff like Guns N' Roses and Metallica," Justin said in an interview with *Seventeen Magazine*.

From a very early age, Justin always loved to sing and make music. "I started playing drums when I was two years old and I got my first drum kit when I was four," he told the BBC. "I basically taught myself to play guitar as well, and later I learned to play trumpet and piano."

HIS EARLY PERFORMANCES

Justin loves to share his gift of music and singing. He has never been shy about performing in front of people. At twelve, he would grab his guitar and busk (entertain on the street for tips) on the front steps of the Avon Theater,

▲ Playing drums came naturally to Justin.

in Stratford, Canada. Tips from tourists and locals would sometimes add up to $150-$200 per day! It was thanks to these tips that Justin was once able to treat his mom to a trip to a Disney theme park.

Around the time that he was a street performer, Justin came in third place in Stratford Star. Stratford Star is a singing competition for youngsters organized by his hometown YMCA. Most articles and interviews say that Justin came in second place; however, the *Toronto Star* states: "It's been widely reported that Bieber came second in the four-week elimination event in Jan. 2007, but youth resource coordinator, Angie Adair, who tallied the votes, said only first prize was announced and that 12-year-old Bieber actually came third behind the two older girls."

On January 19, 2007, twelve-year-old Justin Bieber and his mom logged onto YouTube.com and posted a shaky video of him performing "So Sick" by Ne-Yo. Dressed in a shirt and tie, Justin sings his heart out on a small dark stage. That video received more than 3 million views.

More videos followed, including one of Justin sitting on a couch, strumming his guitar, and singing Justin Timberlake's "Cry Me a River." Below the video are directions on how to pronounce his last name. "Sounds a little like Beeber," his mom wrote.

This way family and friends, who couldn't make it to the Stratford Star show, could see him sing. Little did they know people around the world would be tuning into Justin's videos! Word began to spread about this Canadian cutie with the beautiful singing voice, and millions of views later, life as Justin and his mom knew it was about to change.

JUSTIN GETS DISCOVERED!

Justin told Katie Couric on her @KatieCouric YouTube channel that the first person to e-mail him was from the *Maury* show. His mom didn't think that was the right fit for her son. Soon after, different record companies began contacting Justin, but his mom waited to sign any contracts. One manager kept trying to get Justin and his mom to work with him. This stubborn manager refused to take "no" for an answer. His name is Scott "Scooter" Braun.

◄ *Justin didn't know it at first, but Scooter Braun would help him become a star.*

"We were contacted by Scooter, who is now my manager. He basically stalked us a little bit," Justin told Katie with a smile. "Finally my mom asked him to stop calling us. He said, 'I really see a lot in your son, I can help you guys.' They talked for a couple of hours. He knew some lawyers we could talk to. We ended up flying to Atlanta so he could check us out. We ended up signing a deal with Usher a couple months later."

Justin made it all sound so easy. But there was a bit more to it. Scooter Braun runs his own entertainment company. He was very impressed with Justin's YouTube version of "Respect" by Aretha Franklin. Scooter had helped young Philadelphia-area rapper Asher Roth get a record deal. He was also friendly with famous people like rapper Snoop Dogg. Yes, having Scooter as a manager was great, but Justin still needed to win over important people at the record labels.

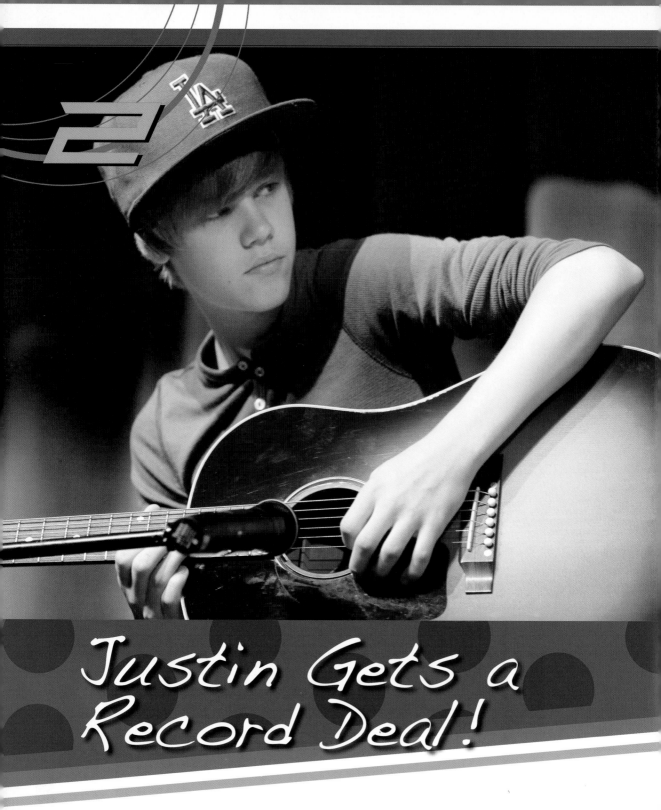

Justin Gets a
Record Deal!

Justin often tells the story behind the first time he flew to Atlanta, Georgia. After a run-in with his idol, Usher, Justin thought for sure he would get to sing for the R&B star. Usher is a Grammy award-winning singer. Like Justin, Usher got his big break as a teenager—he released his first big album at age fifteen.

The first time Justin met Usher, it was simply a case of bad timing. Justin saw Usher pull up at the recording studio and asked if he could do a quick song for him. Usher brushed him off saying, "Sorry little buddy, I just want to get inside, it's cold out here."

Justin was bummed that Usher didn't get to hear him sing during that visit to Atlanta. Justin did, however, get to meet with record label and marketing folks. They were all very impressed with the young and talented Canadian. Scooter sent Justin home with a new video camera.

Scooter had him sing different songs and post them on YouTube to see how many views they would get. Scooter kept an eye on Justin's YouTube video views and Twitter followers. As Justin's online popularity grew, Scooter was sure Justin was going to be a huge success! While Justin

◀ *Justin serenades a group of high school band members in Florida.*

▲ *Usher believed in Justin. He is not just his manager,*
but is also his mentor.

was back in Canada, Scooter couldn't stop raving to Usher about how talented Justin was. Usher saw Justin's YouTube videos and was very impressed. He made plans to fly the young singer back to Atlanta to meet with him. Usher thought Justin had something extra special. "He had two million viewers before I said hello. It was truly his talent . . . Truly his ability to on-the-spot produce that magic," Usher told *Good Morning America Weekend*.

After meeting with Usher, Justin met with another talented Justin—Justin Timberlake. Both Usher and Justin Timberlake were interested in signing him! In the end, Justin went with Usher and Def Jam. "In one corner, I had Usher, Island Def Jam Records and L.A. Reid backing me up. That made me feel good," Justin told Australia's *Herald Sun*.

Usher spoke very highly of Justin on Oprah.com. "I was truly impressed from the moment I saw him. He had a guitar. He could sing. He went over to the piano and could handle himself. He was just so poised. I felt like this kid really has an incredible opportunity to be something and I want to be able to help him and open the doors."

THE BIG MOVE TO ATLANTA

Signing a record deal with Usher and Def Jam in October 2008 meant Justin would have to move. Usher and Scooter's home base is in Atlanta, Georgia. It would be best if Justin was nearby. The young singer didn't seem to mind too much. He'll always have a home in Canada— his grandparents, dad, stepmom and half-siblings still live there. While touring, he once tweeted, "Atlanta! My second home, here we come." While in Atlanta, Usher made sure Justin had all the things a young performer needed. He got Justin a very good vocal coach, a tutor, and someone to assist with his image and style.

Justin is surrounded by people who have his best interest in mind. Scooter and Usher are big brothers to Justin. They are more of a family than just his managers and mentors. Justin even had his invisible braces and dental work done by Scooter's mom. She is a dentist in Connecticut. Like Scooter, Usher takes his job as a role model to Justin seriously. "Sometimes he's like a little brother or a son to me," Usher told *The New York Times*. The two are very close. In fact, Usher gave Justin a Range Rover for his sixteenth birthday and created a special tribute song for him on his seventeenth birthday.

Though busy on the road, Justin did what he had to do to make Atlanta feel like home. He made friends and even dated a local teen model, Caitlin Beadles. Justin and Caitlin no longer date, but they remain close friends. Justin is also very tight with Caitlin's younger brother, Christian. In fact, Christian, an aspiring actor, appears in Justin and Sean Kingston's video for "Eenie Meenie." There are videos of Christian and Justin joking around on YouTube, and they often tweet back and forth to each other.

HIS BIG DEBUT SINGLE

By May 2009, Justin was about to break out in a huge way. People first heard his debut single "One Time" on the radio on May 19 and bought it from iTunes beginning July 7. "One Time" is a song about puppy love, and the video features Justin's real-life friend Ryan Butler. This video wasn't like his other YouTube videos. It was a "real"

▼ *Justin Bieber and Usher have even performed together. Here they perform at Z100's Jingle Ball at New York's Madison Square Garden on December 11, 2009.*

video! "It was really cool going from my webcam to professional videos," Justin told *Billboard*.

The "One Time" video begins with Justin and his friend Ryan playing video games at Usher's house. Usher calls Justin and tells him to kick back and make himself at home—he'll be gone for a bit. Mischievous Justin and his friend get the idea to text message and invite their friends over. This snowballs into a big house party. The video ends with Usher coming home and catching Justin having a little too much fun with his friends. Justin shrugs and gives an innocent smile before the camera fades to black.

As of March 2011, the "One Time" video has reached more than 226 million YouTube views, but that is nothing compared to Justin's video for "Baby," featuring Ludacris. "Baby" has almost 500 million views. Justin describes the "Baby" video: "[it was created in the style of] Michael Jackson's 'The Way You Make Me Feel' video where I'm following her around and trying to get the girl. I'm chasing her and she's really not interested."

◀ *Justin had to attend a VEVO music company party in a leg cast because he had broken his foot. He even performed concerts in the cast!*

Bieber Fever

It's quite ironic that Justin's "Baby" video has him chasing after a girl. In real life, girls are chasing after him! "I like girls chasing me, so it's good," Justin told MTV News referring to MTV's 2010 VMA commercial. The 1960s-style promotional ad featured Justin running from fans. The ad joked that, "Justin Bieber will induce Hysteria."

There is no doubt about it: Justin has an incredible amount of admirers. He lovingly refers to his fans as "Beliebers." Reporters and Justin himself compare his popularity to that of The Beatles. When the EP *My World* (the first of a two-part record release) first came out, it debuted at #6 on the U.S. *Billboard* 200 and sold 137,000 copies the very first week. That was just the beginning of Bieber Fever.

JUSTIN TAKES MANHATTAN

Biebermania officially began on November 20, 2009. Justin was scheduled to sing and meet fans at a preteen clothing store at Roosevelt Field Mall in Garden City, New York.

◄ *Justin sings to a contest winner at the Z100 Jingle Ball on December 11, 2009.*

Nobody expected more than three thousand young fans to line up for the event. For safety reasons, the in-store appearance was canceled. When Justin didn't show, the crowd almost rioted. More than thirty-five policemen were called to break up the chaos. Reports say that five young girls were injured and one adult was arrested.

Fans camp out for days before Justin makes a live appearance or concert tickets go on sale. Video and photos often capture images of young fans sitting on city streets making "I Love Justin" T-shirts and posters. When Justin came to New York City in June 2010 for a live performance on the *Today Show*, more than twelve thousand fans

▲ *Fans use their hands to make hearts to show their love for Justin Bieber before his concert at New York's Madison Square Garden on August, 31, 2010.*

▲ *The crowd at Justin's* Today Show *performance all had Bieber Fever!*

showed up. The adoring fans filled Rockefeller Plaza and the streets surrounding the plaza. Only a thousand were actually allowed into the plaza. Each fan was hoping to meet Justin.

JUSTIN DOWN UNDER

In Australia, there was even more fan frenzy. Justin was set to perform only one live show in Australia in April 2010. More than four thousand fans began pushing and shoving. This caused at least eight injuries. The show was canceled to protect Justin and his fans.

JUSTIN'S MOST MEMORABLE TV MOMENTS

CSI
September 23, 2010, and February 17, 2011: Justin shows off his acting skills as troubled teen Jason McCann.

ELLEN DeGENERES SHOW
October 2, 2009: Wows the audience with a performance of "One Less Lonely Girl." Ellen introduces Justin to two fans who were crying because they didn't make it into the audience.

May 17, 2010: Performs "Baby." Ellen shows Justin hilarious photos of celebs sporting the "Justin flip" hairstyle.

September 12, 2010: Justin answers fans' Twitter questions.

February 23, 2011: Justin gives Ellen a big smooch and shows off his new haircut.

OPRAH
May 11, 2010: Justin opens up to Oprah and performs "Baby."

MTV VIDEO MUSIC AWARDS
September 12, 2010: Justin performs a cool mix of "U Smile," "Baby," and "Somebody to Love" and shows off his drum playing.

Shortly after the Australian incident, Justin arrived at the New Zealand airport. He was shocked to see more than five hundred fans waiting for him. Originally, he planned to sing for them and sign autographs. Security called it off to protect everyone's safety. While Justin and his mom made their way through the airport, his mom was knocked over by excited fans. One fan even grabbed his purple New York

THE TEN MOST FASCINATING PEOPLE OF 2010

December 10, 2010: Justin teaches Barbara Walters how to dance the "dougie."

TODAY SHOW

October 12, 2009: Justin performs "One Time" and "Favorite Girl" live in the Plaza.

June 4, 2010: Performs "Never Say Never" for screaming fans.

Janury 31, 2011: Justin talks about his movie *Never Say Never*.

THE VIEW

March 22, 2010: Answers questions about fame and performs acoustic version of "Never Let You Go."

March 23, 2010: Justin becomes the first celebrity in *The View* history to be brought back for an encore performance.

February 13, 2011: Justin wows fans with an amazing live performance with Jaden Smith and Usher.

Yankees hat. Justin tweeted to fans, "The airport was crazy. Not happy that someone stole my hat and knocked down my mama. Come on people . . . I want to be able to sign and take pics and meet my fans but if you are all pushing, security won't let me."

Today, The View, Saturday Night Live, Jimmy Kimmel, and more have invited Justin to appear as a guest. He's even been on some shows multiple times. They just can't get enough of Biebs! Justin even got a chance to show off his acting skills on TV. Fans loved him on *CSI*.

AN INTERNET SENSATION!

Justin's online popularity grows stronger every day. He is one of the hottest celebrities on Twitter and tweets more than most famous folks. When something or someone is mentioned a lot on Twitter, it becomes a "trend" on the site. Justin was the most popular Twitter trending topic for a long time. The Web site creators caught on to what his fans were up to. In May 2010, the *New York Daily News* reported that Twitter changed its way of figuring out "trending topics." Could it be that Twitter changed its system because of Bieber Fever?

Justin has many followers, fans, and friends on sites like MySpace and Facebook. Justin always keeps fans updated on his whereabouts. He does this with status messages, tweets, and blog posts. "I think the Internet is the best way to reach your fans. A couple of years back, artists didn't have that tool, so why not use it now?" Justin told *Billboard*.

CONNECT TO JUSTIN

Are you connected to Justin?

Twitter: Twitter.com/JustinBieber
Facebook: Facebook.com/JustinBieber
MySpace: MySpace.com/JustinBieber
YouTube Channel: YouTube.com/kidrauhl

EVEN CELEBS HAVE BIEBER FEVER

Drake: "I think he's a talented kid. He has a long, long career ahead of him. I always enjoy watching him do his thing. There are certain people in the industry, just to watch them, the way they move around the room—they just have something special and Justin is one of those kids."

Miley Cyrus: "Bieber fever . . . I'm not necessarily a fan. I don't listen to that kind of music. But my little sister (Noah, 10) was obsessed with him, and he actually gave her a shout-out on Twitter and I thought that was really sweet."

Selena Gomez: "Of course [I have Bieber Fever] I do, absolutely, yes! I love him, he's like my little brother . . . I like to say his name on stage because if I'm performing badly, I say his name and the audience will cheer."

Soccer star David Beckham's sons are Justin fans: "Justin Bieber's the one for them," David Beckham told *Access Hollywood*. "Seeing him perform and seeing the performance he put on— they love him."

Rapper and collaborator on Justin's "Eenie Meenie" song, Sean Kingston: "That's my little bro! I'm gonna support him and be excited for him."

▶ *Justin Bieber and fellow Canadian Drake walk the red carpet at the MuchMusic Video Awards on June 20, 2010.*

▲ Justin Bieber donates money from each of his concerts to charity.

Giving Back

Justin is thankful every day for his success. He uses his popularity to give back to those less fortunate. When he was growing up, his mom struggled to make ends meet. She worked two jobs to support herself and her son. "I grew up with not a lot of money," he told *The New York Times*. "We never owned a house. I want to buy my mom a house." That way of thinking is what makes Justin so giving.

Justin is involved in a wide variety of fund-raisers. From educating needy children in other countries to feeding America's hungry to Haiti relief to even helping rescued animals, Justin does his best to pitch in.

FEEDING THE HUNGRY

Before he became a household name, Justin made a song called "Set a Place at Your Table." The video can be found on his YouTube page. This was one of two songs he sang on a special holiday CD. Money made from the CD went toward a food bank in his hometown.

Justin continues to help feed the hungry. He inspired New York area students to collect tons of food for a radio station contest. Students were encouraged to gather canned foods and dry goods for food banks in New York, New Jersey, and

Connecticut. Long Beach Middle School in Long Beach, New York, collected more than twenty-seven thousand pounds of food and won a private concert!

HELPING HAITI

Justin jumped at the chance to participate in a new version of Michael Jackson and Lionel Richie's "We Are the World 25 for Haiti." Justin, the Jonas Brothers, Miley Cyrus, Kanye West, and Lady Gaga got together to help victims of the earthquake in Haiti. Justin had the honor of singing the first few lines. The new "We Are the World" debuted before the Winter Olympics Opening Ceremony.

Justin also played an important part in the Young Artists For Haiti's version of hip-hop artist K'naan's "Wavin' Flag." The song helped raise money for earthquake recovery in Haiti. Fifty young Canadian performers including Avril Lavigne, Nelly Furtado, Drake, and more contributed their voices. However, Justin's solo seems the most powerful.

Justin delivers the song's only solo and final line: "When I get older/When I get older/I will be stronger just like a wavin' flag." He is the youngest singer involved in the project and was perfect for such sweet song lyrics. Some fans even say the song makes them cry when they hear it. "Wavin' Flag" was released on March 12, 2010. The song held steady for seven weeks on Canadian radio charts and sold more than 160,000 copies on iTunes. More than one million dollars was raised for victims of the Haitian earthquake. Justin was so happy to be a part of the fund-raising efforts that he tweeted, "This is awesome. Canadians helping others. Proud."

JUSTIN HELPS OUT *AMERICAN IDOL*

A few years ago, Justin thought about auditioning for *American Idol*. It wasn't surprising when he got involved in *American Idol*'s *Idol Gives Back* charity show. "Justin's

▼ *Justin helped raise money for the survivors of the Haiti earthquake.*

absolutely phenomenal! He's young and he's a real inspiration for [the] young generation, so it was a really good fit for him to be in that special episode," executive producer Cécile Frot-Coutaz told MTV.

American Idol's *Idol Gives Back* was a telethon. It helped raise money for different causes. Justin appeared on the show with Elton John, Carrie Underwood, Alicia Keys, Black Eyed Peas, and more. Viewers who donated had a chance of winning cool prizes. Proceeds helped charities like Children's Health Fund, Feeding America, Malaria No More, Save the Children and the United Nations Foundation.

PERFORMING FOR PENNIES

Justin teamed up with a New York radio station to help raise the most pennies for charity. Edward Town Middle School, a Buffalo-area school, raised millions of pennies for Justin's radio contest. To thank them, Justin tweeted, "Heading to buffalo and rochester ny tomorrow...they helped me raise over $200k for a children's hospital up there. Incredibly proud of them!" A little while later, Justin added, "Just thought about it...the fans in Buffalo raised $200k in pennies for charity...that is 20 Million Pennies!!! WOW!! VERY PROUD!!"

CLEANING UP THE GULF

On April 20, 2010, the world learned about the largest marine oil spill in history. The oil spill started when an oil rig exploded. Millions of gallons of oil leaked into the ocean, harming and killing sea life.

When Justin heard about the oil spill, he looked for ways to help. Along with other celebrities, he appeared on Larry King's CNN telethon. "Disaster in the Gulf: How You Can Help" aired on June 21 and raised more than $1.8 million for charity.

 "What is going on in the Gulf is a tragedy and we need to help...tune in 2nite to LARRY KING and do what you can.

▼ The 2010 White House Easter Egg Roll was another good cause that Justin lent his voice to. For that year's Egg Roll, President Barack Obama and his wife, Michelle, wanted to promote health in children.

Thanks" Justin tweeted. Afterward, Justin also tweeted Larry King saying, "Just wanted to thank @kingsthings and everyone who donated." He urged fans to keep doing whatever they could to help. "We can still do more!!" Justin tweeted.

A TRUE "PoP" STAR: PENCILS OF PROMISE

Adam Braun created an incredible organization called Pencils of Promise (PoP). Justin was introduced to PoP because his manager, Scooter Braun, is Adam's big brother. PoP brings education to children in areas where school isn't always available. There are areas outside of the United States where kids don't have access to simple things like books, paper, or pencils. By working with local communities, PoP helps build schools.

Justin believes every kid should have the chance to learn. His goal is to have fifteen schools built around the world for children in need. He hopes to do this by donating one dollar from each concert ticket to Pencils of Promise.

Justin continues to come up with ways to raise money and gets involved with many fund-raisers. By giving back and helping others, Justin is a great role model to his fans. Helping others gives Justin a chance to keep it real.

▲ Pencils of Promise founder Adam Braun and Justin Bieber arrive at the Power of Youth event in Hollywood California on October 24, 2010.

Staying True

Justin's spiritual beliefs and close-knit relationship with his family keep the performer down to earth. There are so many ways for young stars to get distracted, harm themselves, or fall in with the wrong crowd. Justin is determined not to go that route. "There are so many kid stars that have fallen down the wrong path and have done the wrong thing. This is a hard business and people just lose themselves." Justin told *ABC News*. "My mom is always there for me and I don't want to let her down."

He also hasn't let fame go to his head. "I think I am [humble]," Justin told CTV. "I think it's very good to surround yourself with people who will not make you feel like you're bigger." When Justin appeared on *Oprah*, he told fans how his mom treats him like a regular kid. "[If I misbehave] my mom takes things away that I really like, like my computer, my phone," he said. "She takes my phone away for a couple of days and I'm like, 'Oh, I need that!'"

BEING HIS OWN PERSON

Fame also hasn't changed Justin's self-image. Reporters or TV personalities often teased him about his former shaggy hairstyle, but Justin just laughed it off and defended his look. "I just kind of liked [my hair], and now people are copying it," Justin told *USA Today*. When he first started out, his management and stylists suggested different looks for him. Justin kept his own look and didn't give in to the pressure.

◀ *Justin Bieber was known for his signature hairstyle.*

AWARDS WON:

2010 MuchMusic Video Awards: Favorite Video "Baby," International Video By A Canadian "Baby," and Favorite New Artist

2010 Teen Choice Awards: Album Pop, Male Artist, Summer Music Star - Male, Breakout Artist Male

2010 MTV Video Awards: Best New Artist

2010 Young Hollywood Awards: Newcomer of the Year

2010 American Music Awards: Breakthrough Artist, Artist of the Year, Pop/Rock Album, Pop/Rock Male Artist

NOMINATED:

2010 BET: Best New Artist

2010 Juno Awards: Album of the Year, Pop Album of the Year, and New Artist of the Year

2010 Teen Choice Awards: Most Fanatic Fans

2011 Grammy Awards: Best New Artist, Best Pop Vocal Album

"I wasn't sure that was going to work, but he was adamant that this was going to be part of his image," Usher added. "I like that he stands up for himself, but also is very open to direction." Justin also feels this way when it comes to his clothing style. Although his road manager assists him with his wardrobe, Justin has full control of what he wears.

▲ *Not only did Justin win four American Music Awards in 2010, but he also performed at the show.*

REMEMBERING HIS ROOTS

"Three years ago I was on the side of the street busking in Stratford for anyone who would listen," Justin tweeted after a sold-out concert at the Air Canada Centre. "2nite we sold out the ACC!! NEVER SAY NEVER!" A few hours later he added, "2nite goes out to all the small town kids! I'm one of u … We are all living a dream right now and it can happen."

Justin's rise to the top is special because he didn't come from a wealthy family. "I grew up below the poverty line," Justin told ShowbizSpy.com. "It made me stronger." He wasn't a Disney or Nickelodeon actor-turned-singer like many other celebrities. He didn't have famous parents. He didn't have a relative in the music business.

Justin is proof that a talented kid from a small town can make it big. He believes that hard work, dedication, and believing in oneself really can make dreams come true. "I think coming from Stratford, Ontario, basically gives others hope," Justin told CTA News. "I came from a place where nobody has ever come from and I'm now known worldwide."

"BIEBS" STAYS BUSY

Between being tutored and rehearsing with his vocal coach, Justin works very hard to achieve his goals. Justin's dedication hasn't gone unnoticed—*Forbes* magazine included him in their "11 Most Successful Teen Celebrity

Entrepreneurs" list. Justin has big plans, including two feature films, a new version of MTV's hit show *Punk'd*, TV appearances, a new perfume/cologne, concerts, and much more.

The singer's long-awaited 3-D feature film *Never Say Never* includes behind-the-scenes clips, live performances, interviews with his management, and vintage home video of Justin throughout the years. *Never Say Never* hit American theaters on February 11, 2011, and gave fans hope that anything is possible if they follow their hearts and "never say never." In addition to this biographical movie, Justin will begin shooting a fictional film with Will Smith in mid-2011.

Turning his talent to TV, there is talk that Justin will be hosting episodes of MTV's *Punk'd*. Along with Ashton Kutcher—the show's producer and star—Justin would begin the first half of the *Punk'd* season by taking part in the actual "punking" of fellow celebs. As time goes by, Justin's role may get smaller and have him just introducing the practical jokes.

Justin has teamed up with Give Back Brands to make a new scent for his fans with proceeds going toward charity. "I want to create something that will have the girls go crazy," Justin joked with *People* magazine. "Most male celebrities do male colognes for other males. I think that me making a female fragrance is just a different idea, and I think it's going to be successful."

Justin hopes to collaborate with some of his favorite artists, tour the world, and more. During an interview with Canadian TV, he summed up his future nicely: "I'm going to be a career artist," he said. "Five years down the road, I see myself furthering my career. Maybe winning a Grammy, starring in a movie." In fact, less than a year after saying this, Justin was indeed nominated for two Grammy awards. Even though he didn't win, this was a huge feat for such a young star. It's obvious that Justin will remain in the spotlight for a very long time.

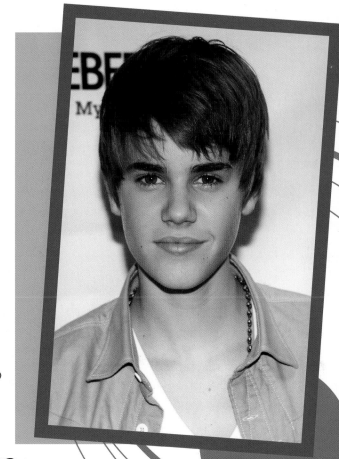

▶ *Justin Bieber is a big star who will stay in the spotlight.*

Timeline

1994 Justin Drew Bieber is born on March 1 in Ontario, Canada.

2007 Justin and his mom post his videos on YouTube.

2008 Justin signs a record contract with Island Def Jam Records in October.

2009 His first single "One Time" is released to radio in May.

2009 Signs up for Twitter in June having no idea he'll be a Twitter trending phenomenon.

2009 November: Justin's debut CD, *My World*, EP released and a near-riot breaks out at a Long Island mall.

2009 March: Justin's full studio version *My World* CD is released, and his *My World* tour is announced.

2010 Makes history as one of the youngest celebrities to perform on *SNL* in April.

2010 Kicks off first-ever major headlining tour in June.

2010 He wins four Teen Choice awards in August.

2010 Wins four American Music Awards in November.

2011 Justin's 3D movie *Never Say Never* opens in theaters on February 11.

2011 Ellen Degeneres raises $40,000 for an animal charity by auctioning off a lock of Justin's hair on March 2.

Further Info

Books

Bieber, Justin. *Justin Bieber*: *First Step 2 Forever: My Story*. New York: HarperCollins Children's Books, 2010.

Parker, Evie. *100% Justin Bieber: The Unofficial Biography*. New York: Bantam Books, 2010.

Parvis, Sarah. *Justin Bieber*. Kansas City, Miss.: Andrews McMeel Publishing LLC, 2010.

DVDs

Justin Bieber: Never Say Never

Internet Addresses

Bieber Fever
The official site for Justin Bieber fans is for paid members only.

http://bieberfever.com/

Justin Bieber
Justin Bieber's official Web site

http://www.justinbiebermusic.com/

Discography

CDs
November 17, 2009: *My World EP*
March 23, 2010: *My World 2.0*
November 26, 2010: *My Worlds Acoustic*
February 14, 2011: *Never Say Never — The Remixes*

Singles
July 2009: "One Time"
October 2009: "One Less Lonely Girl"
October 2009: "Love Me"
November 2009: "Favorite Girl"
January 2010: "Baby," with Ludacris
March 2010: "Never Let You Go"

March 2010: "U Smile"
April 2010: "Somebody to Love"
June 2010: "Never Say Never" featuring Jaden Smith
June 2010: "Somebody to Love" remix featuring Usher
November 2010: "Pray"

Singles Featuring Justin
February 2010: "We Are The World 25 for Haiti"
March 2010: "Wavin' Flag" Young Artists for Haiti
March 2010: "Eenie Meenie" Sean Kingston

Glossary

busk—To entertain, sing, or perform for people on the street or in a public place for tips.

collaborate—Work with another person as a team or partner.

contract—A legal understanding that people agree upon and sign before working together.

ironic—When events have a result that is opposite to what was expected.

manager—Someone who guides and oversees career decisions.

mentor—A wise or trusted teacher, leader, or role model.

R&B—Rhythm and blues; a style of urban music that usually has strong repetition and simple melodies.

Twitter—A Web site where people communicate with each other, celebrities, and popular companies or brands in the form of messages called "tweets."

Twitter followers—Twitter users who choose to receive the messages of another Twitter member.

Index